The **Rap** Scene

The Stars ♪ The Fans ♪ The Music

Sarah W. Moore

 Enslow Publishers, Inc.
40 Industrial Road
Box 398
Berkeley Heights, NJ 07922
USA

http://www.enslow.com

Library of Congress Cataloging-in-Publication Data

Moore, Sarah W.
  The rap scene : the stars, the fans, the music / Sarah W. Moore.
    p. cm. — (The music scene)
  Includes bibliographical references and index.
  Summary: "Read about the music, stars, clothes, contracts, and world of rap
music"—Provided by publisher.
  ISBN-13: 978-0-7660-3397-9
  ISBN-10: 0-7660-3397-X
  1. Rap (Music)—History and criticism—Juvenile literature. I. Title.
  ML3531.M66 2009
  782.421649—dc22

                      2008048011

Printed in the United States of America

10 9 8 7 6 5 4 3 2 1

To Our Readers:
This text has not been authorized by the musicians or bands mentioned
throughout this book.

    We have done our best to make sure all Internet addresses in this book
were active and appropriate when we went to press. However, the author and
the publisher have no control over and assume no liability for the material
available on those Internet sites or on other Web sites they may link to. Any
comments or suggestions can be sent by e-mail to comments@enslow.com
or to the address on the back cover.

♻ Enslow Publishers, Inc., is committed to printing our books on recycled
paper. The paper in every book contains 10% to 30% post-consumer waste
(PCW). The cover board on the outside of each book contains 100%
PCW. Our goal is to do our part to help young people and the
environment too!

Cover Photo Credit: Getty Images/Karl Walter
Interior Photo Credits: Alamy/Content Mine International, p. 5;
Alamy/Inti St. Clair/Blend Images, p. 19; Alamy/Image Source
Pink, p. 35; Alamy/Jupiter Images/Thinkstock, p. 40; AP Photo/
Adam Hunger, pp. 1, 38; AP Photo/Mark J. Terrill, p. 4; AP Photo/
Lee Jin-man, p. 12; AP Photo/Damian Dovarganes, p. 17; AP
Photo/Jim Cooper, p. 34; Corbis/Rob McEwan/Columbia Pictures
rel/Bureau L.A. Collection, p. 21; Corbis/David Bergman, p. 36;
Getty Images/Rocky Widner/NBAE, p. 6; Getty Images/Bryan
Bedder, p. 13; Getty Images/Frank Micelotta, p. 16; Getty Images/
Mario Tama, p. 24; Getty Images/Chris Walter/WireImage, p. 28;
iStockphoto.com/Dejan Ljami, p. 41; Retna Ltd./Robb D. Cohen, p. 2;
Retna Ltd./Janette Beckman, p. 8; Retna Ltd./John Ricard, p. 9; Retna
Ltd./Zach Cordner, p. 10; Retna Ltd./Jennifer Maler, p. 11; Retna Ltd./
David Atlas, p. 14; Retna Ltd./Zach Cordner, p. 15; Retna Ltd./Adrian
Boot, p. 22; Retna Ltd./Janette Beckman, pp. 23, 25; Retna Ltd./Tara
Canova, p. 26; Retna Ltd./Brian Hineline, p. 29; Retna Ltd./Michael
Benabib, p. 31; Retna Ltd./Lula Camus, p. 32.

*Cover: Jay-Z performs in Hollywood,
California, in 2006.*

*Right: Busta Rhymes raps at the Fox
Theatre in Atlanta, Georgia.*

Contents

① *Hot Stuff*

Rap music is just about everywhere. It's in movies and on television. It's pumping out of cars cruising down the road. Rap influences our whole culture—and fans like you make it all possible!

HOT *Rappers*

Lil Wayne is a hot rapper. Raised in New Orleans, Lil Wayne started recording albums when he was a teenager. Recently, a writer from the magazine *Rolling Stone* called Lil Wayne "the best rapper alive."[1]

Snoop Dogg is a major player in the rap industry. He overcame hard times as a kid. Now he is one of the most respected rap artists in the world.

Lil Wayne accepts the Grammy Award for Best Rap Album in February 2009.

Women *Rule*

Rapper **Missy Elliott** is known for her unique style and dedication to charity work. She has sold more records than any other female rapper.[2] Elliott often encourages young people to do well in school. She jokes, "If I didn't have some kind of education, then I wouldn't be able to count my money."[3]

Missy Elliott performs in Amsterdam, a major European city.

RAP
Around the World

You can find rap stars all around the world. Rap has deep roots in Africa. **Wass-Wong** is a group from Niger. Their name means "message from the warriors."[4] Also listen for artists like **Hilltop Woods** from Australia, Mexico's **Control Machete**, and **XXX Rottweiler hundar** of Iceland.

2 "I'm Your Biggest Fan!"

Young people especially like rap music. They love the fast-paced beats and rhyming words. Rap fans relate to the lyrics, or words, of rap music.

They get to know the cool slang that rappers use in their rhymes. Then they use rap to express themselves.

Back in the Day

The first rap artists and fans were African Americans in New York City's South Bronx neighborhood. In his book *Can't Stop Won't Stop*, author Jeff Chang says that rap started with **DJ Kool Herc** and his parties in the early 1970s. Herc would act as the DJ, playing music and talking into a microphone at the same time. Fans started to like the combination of spoken words and music.

Keeping It Real

Rap also began as a way for African Americans to express themselves and their culture. Over time, people of many other cultural groups— Asian, Latino, white, and more—adopted rap. Today, rap's rhymes and rhythms reach fans of all ages and backgrounds. From the streets of major American cities to fan sites on the Internet, people are listening to rap music.

3 *Ultimate Style*

Clothing is a big part of what defines rap music. Rap styles have gone on to influence the entire fashion world.

Old *School*

The style of the 1980s is now called old school. Artists like **N.W.A.** and **2 Live Crew** wore baggy pants, sneakers with fat laces, thick gold or silver chains, baseball hats, sunglasses, and track or Starter jackets.

In the 1990s, rappers like **D'Angelo** and **Tupac** went shirtless and wore gold chains. Large clock necklaces were also hot. Some members of **Public Enemy** topped their heads with French hats called berets.

The members of 2 Live Crew helped create rap's old school style of fashion.

New
School

Today's new school rappers combine old and new styles. They still wear large chains and sunglasses. *Lil Wayne* often goes shirtless. *50 Cent* wears white tank tops. Other stars like *Kanye West* go for collared shirts and blazers. *Missy Elliott* prefers old school baggy pants and tracksuits.

Many rap artists like to appear wealthy, so they load themselves up with bling—large necklaces, rings, and other jewelry. Rappers call their shoes kicks. Asics, Adidas, and Pumas have always been popular. Rappers and their fans also wear all kinds of hats. Members of *Run-DMC* wear a bowler. *Aesop Rock* wears a baseball cap.

Hot new rapper Lil Mama represents the new school: updated clothes mixed with plenty of bling.

The Whole Picture

Style is much more than just clothing. Some rappers wear their hair in cornrows or dreadlocks. Cornrows are small braids in even rows. Dreadlocks are tightly wound knots of hair. Some rappers wear grills—pieces of gold or platinum that sit on top of the teeth. Even cars are part of the image. Many rappers have souped-up "rides." Chevrolets and Cadillacs turn into lowriders with air pumps that can lift the car and make it bounce up and down.

Clothing is just one part of a rapper's image. Hair styles are important, too. Here, *Ludacris* wears his hair in cornrows at a concert in Anaheim, California.

Famous graffiti artists show their work at a block party in New York City.

Rapping with Paint

Graffiti—urban street art—is an art form using spray paint or markers to create letters, words, and pictures. Graffiti is a visual expression of rap music. Sometimes people paint graffiti illegally, but many artists use their own materials. A recent exhibit at the Brooklyn Museum in New York City featured graffiti artists.[5]

Rap's dance styles have caught on worldwide. Here, a break-dancer defies gravity at a competition in South Korea.

4 Dance!

From playgrounds to basketball courts at halftime, dancing is an exciting part of rap music. People dance in clubs. Fans wave their hands in the air and sway their hips to the beat.

A break is part of a rap song with a strong rhythm. DJs sometimes put together the breaks of different songs. This creates a long and fast rhythm section for dancers to move to.

In the Break
Break dancing came from a 1970s street movement in New York City. Break dancing is still popular today. The moves look like acrobatics, and they're a great workout!

Soulja Boy Dance
The Soulja Boy Dance is very popular. This dance is a set of fun moves to **Soulja Boy**'s catchy song "Crank That (Soulja Boy)." On MTV's show *Total Request Live*, Soulja Boy taught his dance to movie star Natalie Portman.

Live on MTV, Soulja Boy brings actress Natalie Portman up to date on the Soulja Boy Dance.

Lil Wayne shows off his instrumental talent at a concert in New Jersey.

5 On the Road

Touring is thrilling. Traveling musicians get excited to arrive in a new town and to share their music with new fans. Many rappers pick up a souvenir from every place they visit.[6] Successful rappers usually have a tour bus. The bus is like a hotel, complete with beds and bathrooms.

But being on tour can also be really tiring. Some artists are so busy that they forget what day of the week it is! Rap artists play at clubs, arenas, and other places around the country and across the world. New artists start out at small clubs or house parties. Popular rappers play at large stadiums.

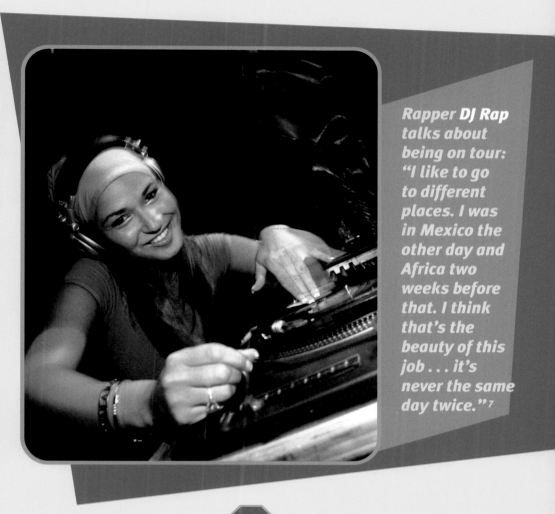

*Rapper **DJ Rap** talks about being on tour: "I like to go to different places. I was in Mexico the other day and Africa two weeks before that. I think that's the beauty of this job . . . it's never the same day twice."* [7]

Nothing beats the energy of a live rap show. Here, Kanye West gets close to his fans on stage in Detroit, Michigan.

6 Live!

Going to a live rap show is different from listening to a recording. You can see colored lights, special effects, and dancers in costumes. Some artists use big movie screens to show pictures or movies as they perform. Many rappers dance as they sing, and the whole audience often dances along. You can't help but feel the excitement!

Watch Your Ears!

Live music is intense, so you have to be aware. Some shows are so loud that they cause long-term damage to the ears. Always bring a pair of earplugs to a live performance.[8] In 2005, rapper *Foxy Brown* suffered hearing loss from being around loud music. Brown's hearing loss was treatable—through painful surgery—but some hearing loss can be permanent.[9]

Joining In

Another exciting part of seeing a live show is meeting other fans. You can make friends who have the same interests as yours. Rap music has a way of bringing people together.

A group of high school students works together to send a message to their favorite artist.

7 *Ear Candy*

How can you get your hands on some rap music?
First, make sure a parent or trusted adult approves of the music you listen to. Some rap music is inappropriate for kids or teenagers.

On the *Waves*

The cheapest way to listen to rap is on the radio. Radio stations play some of the hottest new rap music. One problem is that you don't get to choose the songs you hear. Also, you might not want to listen to all the commercials. Some satellite radio services are commercial-free, but you have to pay for them.

Rap on the Web
A great way to find new rappers is on social networking Web sites, such as MySpace. On these sites you can listen to sample songs for free. Some rap artists offer free music on their personal Web sites. Start listening!

Albums

You can buy rap CDs at a store or on the Internet. You can also buy MP3 files and keep them on your computer or MP3 player. Just be sure to follow the rules. It is illegal to download music without paying for it—unless an artist says it is free. Illegal downloading is called music piracy. Making copies of CDs is also illegal.

8 *On the Big Screen*

Rap has a major influence on the movie industry. Movies today show the people, music, and dancing of the rap scene. Many movies have rap music on their soundtracks. Rap adds excitement and raw energy to the screen.

Ice Cube Heats Up the Screen

Boys in the Hood, named after Eazy-E's song "Boyz-n-the-Hood," explores the struggles of urban life and the roots of rap. The cast includes rapper **Ice Cube**. Ice Cube has many careers. He also directs and produces films and writes screenplays.

Eminem's Story

8 Mile is a movie starring **Eminem**. It shows many features of rap, including battle rapping. Battle rapping is when two or more rappers compete against each other to come up with the best rhymes. Many people think *8 Mile* is

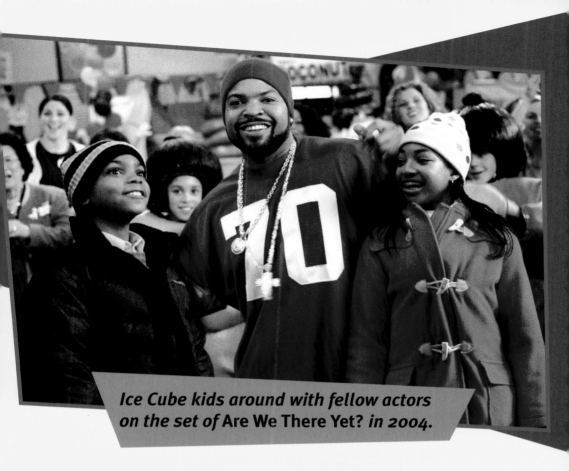

Ice Cube kids around with fellow actors on the set of Are We There Yet? *in 2004.*

an autobiography because many events in the movie happened in Eminem's life.

Crossover Stars

Other rappers who have made it in Hollywood are **Queen Latifah** (*Hairspray, Ice Age,* and *Taxi*), **LL Cool J** (*Charlie's Angels* and *Toys*), and **Will Smith** (*Men in Black* and *Hancock*). *Men in Black* made over $500 million at the box office! This movie is about two officers who protect Earth from aliens.

9 First Moments

People disagree about who started rap music.
Afrika Bambaataa says that he and *Grandmaster*
Flash first created rap in the South Bronx (a
part of New York City) in the late 1970s.[10] *Russell*
Simmons is known as the Godfather of Rap.
Simmons agrees that rap started in the Bronx.

Other people say that the first rap song was
"Here Come the Judge" by comedian *Pigmeat*
Markham in 1968.[11] *DJ Kool Herc* claims that rap
began in dance clubs. Some of the first DJs
would say things into the
microphone like "Clap
your hands" or "You all
ready to party?"

Grandmaster Flash helped
invent rap in New York
City in the late 1970s.

Floats Like a Butterfly . . .

Rapping, or speaking in short rhymes, goes back to African-American jazz musicians and rhythm and blues DJs. In the 1960s and 1970s, famous black boxers like Muhammad Ali would speak in short, catchy phrases to scare their opponents. Ali was known to say that he "floats like a butterfly, stings like a bee."

Mainstream?

Whatever its first moments were, rap began as a rebellion against other music. Disco and dance music were popular at the time. Rappers gave live shows before they started producing records.[12] Little did they know that rap would enter the mainstream— in a big way!

The Infinity Rappers were on the scene in 1982.

These dolls are just one example of how rap culture has turned into a worldwide marketing sensation.

10 Spreading Like Wildfire

Rap music has been a wild success since the 1970s. As the record industry introduced newer and younger rappers, the music appealed to more and younger fans. Today, record companies market rap in many ways. One way is to create products such as toy microphones. The products help spread the music—and the entire rap culture.

Music TV

MTV helped spread rap music all over the world. In the 1980s, rap began influencing pop music. The first song to include rapping by a non-black artist was **Debbie Harry**'s "Rapture." The first major female rap group was **Salt-N-Pepa**. Their music soared on the Top 40 Charts. Salt-N-Pepa's first hit was in 1985, and they kept making great music into the 1990s.[13] Starting in the 1980s, the **Beastie Boys**' pop hits helped spread rap to white audiences.

Many video games have rap music on their soundtracks. Fans also learn more about rap when they read magazines such as Vibe, The Source, *and* Downlow Magazine. *Characters on TV shows, such as* The Simpsons, *talk about rap culture.*

Salt-N-Pepa was the first major female rap group. They were riding a wave of fame when this picture was taken in 1988.

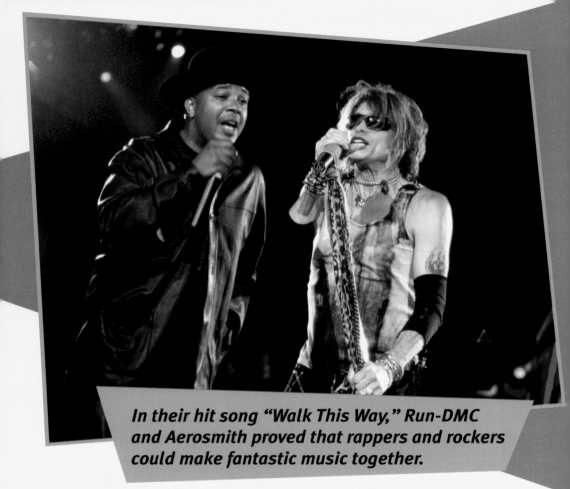

In their hit song "Walk This Way," Run-DMC and Aerosmith proved that rappers and rockers could make fantastic music together.

11 Not So Simple

There are many different types of rap. Gangsta rap became popular in the 1990s. Some gangsta rap is about illegal and dangerous activities. Be careful about this type of rap. Get permission from your parents or a trusted adult before listening to gangsta rap artists.

Powerful Blends

Rap also gets blended with pop music or rock and roll. An example of this combination is **Run-DMC**'s "Walk This Way" (1986), a version of a song by the rock band **Aerosmith**. This song won the Soul Train Music Award for Best Rap Single.[14] **Gwen Stefani** of the popular band **No Doubt** released the single "Hollaback Girl" in 2005. This song blends pop and rap.

A rapper who tells a story with his rhymes is doing concept rap. Freestyle rappers make up rhymes on the spot and often duel with each other. Grime is a type of rap that has robotic beats while the rapper rhymes.

International Rhymes

Rap reaches far outside the United States. From Jamaica comes dancehall, a type of pop music with rapping over the rhythm. Bhangra music, from India, combines reggae and hip-hop. An example of the bhangra sound is **Jay-Z** and **Panjabi MC**'s "Beware the Boys." The Netherlands has its own kind of rap, called Nederhop. Portuguese people call their rap music hip-hop tuga. British artists slow the beat down and sing along. This is called trip hop.

The murders of Biggie Smalls (shown here) and Tupac Shakur came in a dark period in the history of rap.

12 Friendly—and Not So Friendly—Rivalries

Some rappers develop rivalries, or competitions, with each other. This started in the South Bronx, where rappers would "battle" each other to see who had the best rhymes. One of the most famous rap rivalries was the East Coast (Bad Boy Records) versus West Coast (Death Row Records) fight. Rappers would make mean comments about rivals in their songs. In 1996 and 1997, artists *Biggie Smalls* and *Tupac Shakur* were murdered. Their cases are unsolved, but most people believe their murders were connected to the rivalry.

The murders put an end to the rivalry, but the fighting damaged the reputations of the record companies. This opened ground for new rappers. **Dr. Dre** left Death Row Records to form his own major rap label, Aftermath Entertainment. Many great albums, like **Busta Rhymes**'s *The Big Bang*, have come out of this record company.

Slammin' Rhymes
Poetry slams are friendly ways to compete with the spoken word. Poetry slams come from the idea of battle rapping. But instead of rapping, kids read or recite poetry to see who has the best skills. It is a great way to get creative and involved!

Speak for the Title

Battle rapping is a type of friendly rivalry. Anyone from beginners to stars can battle rap. When performing on stage, two or more rappers try to outrhyme each other. Often the rappers make fun of each other in a friendly way while rhyming. The raps that get the best audience feedback are the winners.

Busta Rhymes raps his heart out at a concert in 2008.

13 *The Studios*

A studio is a place where people record music. Instead of looking for popular studios, rappers usually search for the best producers and go to them. Some of the best producers, like **Dr. Dre** and **Ice Cube**, started out as rappers. **Kanye West**, the **Neptunes**, and **Timbaland**, on the other hand, began their careers as producers.

Dr. Dre

One of rap's most famous and influential producers, **Dr. Dre** has his own house studio. He discovered **Snoop Dogg** and **Eminem**. Dre also engineered **50 Cent**'s album *Get Rich or Die Tryin'.* Dre says, "One of the things I like most about producing is recording vocals. I like instructing people, but I'm also trying to bring out a good performance, so I work with them—encourage them."[15]

Dynamic Duo: Timbaland and Missy Elliott

Producer Timbaland and **Missy Elliott** were childhood friends. Elliott really liked the music

Timbaland made with rapper **Magoo**, so she invited him to audition for a group. Soon Elliott, Timbaland, and Magoo were all part of **Da Basement Crew**. Timbaland went on to produce Elliott's popular album *Supa Dupa Fly*.

Powerful rap producer Timbaland works in his studio.

14 Tale of a Contract

Rappers who want to be famous need to score a record contract. A contract gives them money to make records in a studio, to go on tour, and to show up at fun events.

Music is a big-money business. The successful rappers are the ones with good agents. An agent is a professional who is paid to represent an artist. Agents use their contacts to take a rapper's career to the

British rapper Lady Sovereign onthe set of the video for her song"Save the Hoodie"

next level. They try to line up concerts at larger venues. They also help rappers sign record contracts.

A Tale of Discovery

Lady Sovereign, a rapper from England, has an exciting record contract story. She started rapping at age fourteen. Lady Sovereign convinced one producer to let her write the music for a movie. An album producer listened to the soundtrack and liked what he heard. He invited Lady Sovereign to rap on a new CD called *The Battle*. Released in 2003, the CD is a freestyle battle rap between a female and a male artist.

The Road to Stardom

The Battle was a hit. Producer **Jay-Z** liked the CD and signed Lady Sovereign to his labels Def Jam and Roc-a-Fella Records. She recorded another album called *Public Warning* (2006). Soon after the album's release, Lady Sovereign performed on *The Late Show with David Letterman*.

15 Take One!

Recording an album in a studio is a difficult process. Songs are rarely perfect on the first try. Musicians spend long days in the studio. They lay down tracks one by one. This means they record each instrument or voice separately. Sometimes a rapper has to rap his part several times before he gets everything just right.

Note-Perfect

The engineers make sure all the volume levels are perfect. Then they mix the tracks into a whole song. At this time, engineers can add in more samples or edits. Then the record gets mastered. This process sets all the songs at the same volume.

Engineers use lots of tricks in the studio. They use electronic effects such as reverb and delay. Reverb is the process of letting echoes build up. Delay means recording a sound and playing it back later. Sampling is a way of putting a section of older music into new songs.

Producer Dr. Dre does not like the use of sampling. He says, "I want to be known as the producer's producer. The cellos are real. I don't use samples. I may hear something I like on an old record that may inspire me, but I'd rather use musicians to recreate the sound or elaborate on it. I can control it better."[16]

With human intelligence and high-tech equipment, today's producers have endless tricks up their sleeve.

16 Rap Music in Action

Jay-Z, a rapper known for giving back to the community, performs at the Live 8 benefit concert in 2005.

Many people in the rap industry use their success to give back to the community. Rappers work to solve world problems like hunger, AIDS, global warming, and violence. They organize benefit concerts such as Live 8, Rock for Darfur, and Live Earth. Stars raise a lot of money for their causes. They also use their music to teach young people about important social issues. For example, **Kenya** wrote a rap to stop the disease AIDS.

Costly Diamonds
Kanye West wanted to change the idea that rappers only want wealth and "bling." He learned about West African children who were being forced to mine for diamonds. In 2005, West released "Diamonds from Sierra Leone." The song helped educate people about the terrible working conditions in diamond fields.

Water for Life

Rapper **Jay-Z** decided to teach kids about the issue of water shortage. He made a documentary about places in the world that do not have enough water. He called the movie *The Diary of Jay-Z: Water for Life*. He also went on tour for the cause. With the money he made, he paid for water pumps and storage equipment in Africa. Schools and libraries show Jay-Z's documentary to kids.[17]

College students take a class in turntable techniques.

17 *Get into It*

You don't have to be a professional to learn how to rap! Lots of kids get together with friends to make a rap group. Many successful rappers started by rapping with their friends. The more you practice, the easier it is to freestyle. Rhyming one phrase with the next takes some work.

Tech Tricks

You can use a computer program or a Web site to make your own raps and beats. For example, on some video games, players rap along with several tracks of beats.

Rap School

Music lessons are another way to get into rap. Try learning how to beatbox. Beatboxing is making a beat and other sounds with your mouth. Or get your hands on some turntables. Turntables are two record players side by side. You can put together two sounds from two different records to make a new song. Or, you can use two of the same records to mix a song in a new way. DJs use turntables to scratch old records. Scratching is a cool way to make rhythmic sounds.

Are you way into words? Enter a rap, jam, or poetry contest. You can even find a local studio and record a CD. The possibilities are endless! What do you want to do?

For a Living

The rap industry always has room for new talent. That talent could be you!

There are lots of different jobs in the rap industry. Sure, you can become a rapper, but there's more! Imagine a career as an engineer or producer of rap albums. Or you might work for a record label or marketing firm. These employees line up interviews and plan a rapper's schedule of appearances. Yet another rap job is reviewing CDs and concerts for magazines or Web sites.

Many record companies have "street teams." These are groups of young people who help to promote an artist or performance. Artists, fashion designers, lawyers, movie and TV producers, and journalists also make a living in the rap industry.

The rap scene is wide open and waiting for you!

Hey Mister DJ!

Professional DJs spin records at clubs, weddings, parties, and other places. DJing can pay pretty well. Other DJs work for radio stations. They get to host events and meet famous artists.

Glossary

agent—Someone who represents musicians by getting shows and record deals for them.

autobiography—A book or movie that a person creates about his or her own life.

battle rapping—Rapping in which two or more rappers face off and try to out-rhyme each other.

beatbox—To make rhythmic sounds with the mouth.

bling—Flashy jewelry and other accessories (comes from "bling-bling").

culture—The way of life of a group of people.

delay—A sound that is recorded and played back later.

engineers—People who control recording equipment in a studio.

graffiti—Images or words scratched, painted, or marked onto a building or other object.

grills—Pieces of metal jewelry that are worn over teeth.

lowriders—Cars that are modified to sit low to the ground.

lyrics—The words of a song.

music piracy—The illegal downloading or copying of music.

old school rap—Early rap recorded from the 1970s to the 1990s; rap culture from that time.

producer—The person in charge of recording an album.

rebellion—An outbreak or protest against authority.

reverb—The effect of echoes on a recording.

rhythm—The beat or pulse of a song.

rivalries—Competitions that often last a long time.

sampling—Using previously recorded pieces of music to create new songs.

scratch—To make a harsh noise by moving a record back and forth on a moving turntable.

slang—Informal language, often used by young people.

turntables—Sets of two record players.

Time Line

1956 DJs begin toasting (rapping) over Jamaican beats.

1969 Ice Cube is born in Los Angeles.

1979 The Sugarhill Gang releases "Rapper's Delight."

1982 Grandmaster Flash and the Furious Five release "The Message."

1983 Gangsta rap starts with the release of Ice T's *Cold Winter Madness*.

1986 Run-DMC and Aerosmith work together to record "Walk This Way."

1988 N.W.A. releases *Straight Outta Compton*.

1991 Ice Cube stars in *Boyz N the Hood*.

1992 Dr. Dre and Suge Knight form Death Row Records.

1993 Salt-N-Pepa releases *Very Necessary*, the best-selling rap album by a female artist.

1994 Rappers Biggie Smalls and Tupac Shakur meet and record songs together.

1997 Will Smith stars in the movie *Men in Black*.

1999 Jay-Z, DMX, Redman, and Method Man begin their Hard Knock Life Tour, the first successful rap tour in a decade.

2000 Eminem releases *The Marshall Mathers EP*, one of the best-selling rap records of all time.

2003 Outkast's *Speakerboxxx/the Love Below* wins the Grammy Award for Best Album of the Year.

2005 Nelly stars in *The Longest Yard* with Adam Sandler and Chris Rock.

2006 Kanye West wins Grammy Awards for Best Rap Album and Best Rap Song.

2007 Soulja Boy's "Crank That (Soulja Boy)" reaches number one on the Billboard 100 Charts.

2008 Lil Wayne releases *Tha Carter III*, which wins a Grammy Award for Best Rap Album.

End Notes

1. Jody Rosen, "Lil Wayne: *Tha Carter III*," *Rolling Stone*, June 26, 2008, <http://www.rollingstone.com/reviews/album/21080575/review/21127308/tha_carter_iii> (February 11, 2009).

2. Margeaux Watson, "Rhymes and Reasons," *EW.com*, September 15, 2006, <http://www.ew.com/ew/article/0,,1535082,00.html> (February 11, 2009).

3. Missy Elliott, "Missy Elliott Quotes," *Thinkexist.com*, n.d., <http://thinkexist.com/quotes/missy_elliott/> (February 11, 2009).

4. "Wass-Wong," *African-Rap.com*, n.d., <http://www.african-rap.com/artists/wass-wong.html> (February 11, 2009).

5. "Exhibitions: Graffiti," *Brooklyn Museum*, n.d., <http://www.brooklynmuseum.org/exhibitions/graffiti/> (February 11, 2009).

6. DJ Mars, "Tour Diary: DJ Mars," *Vibe*, June 7, 2007, <http://www.vibe.com/news/online_exclusives/2007/06/dj_mars_tour_diary/> (February 11, 2009).

7. John Brassil, "DJ Rap Interview," *About.com*, n.d., <http://dancemusic.about.com/cs/interviews/a/DJRapInt.htm> (February 11, 2009).

8. Stephen Manning, "Imagination Stage Casts Deaf Performers in Hip-hop Show," *4HearingLoss*, March 2, 2006, <http://www.4hearingloss.com/archives/2006/03/imagination_sta.html> (February 11, 2009).

9. "Foxy Brown Comments on Hearing Loss," *Hip Hop Reaction*, December 17, 2005, <http://www.hiphopreaction.com/news/Foxy-Brown-comments-on-hearing-loss> (February 11, 2009).

10. "The Music World of Afrika Bambaataa," *Universal Zulu Nation*, n.d., <http://www.zulunation.com/afrika.html> (February 11, 2009).

11. Mark Deming, "Pigmeat Markham Biography," *Artist Direct*, n.d., <http://www.artistdirect.com/nad/music/artist/bio/0,,463454,00.html> (February 11, 2009).

12. Kwaku Person-Lynn, Ph.D., "The Origin of Rap," *Africa Within*, June 29, 2001, <http://www.africawithin.com/kwaku/origin_of_rap.htm> (February 11, 2009).

13. "Bio," *Salt Unrapped*, n.d., <http://www.saltunrapped.com/> (February 11, 2009).

14. "1986 Soul Train Music Awards," *metrolyrics*, n.d., <http://www.metrolyrics.com/1986-soul-train-music-awards.html> (February 11, 2009).

15. Josh Tyrangiel, "In the Doctor's House," *Time*, n.d., <http://www.time.com/time/musicgoesglobal/na/mdre.html> (February 11, 2009).

16. Ibid.

17. Elena Gorgan, "Jay-Z, To Rap for Water Crisis Awareness," *Softpedia*, August 10, 2006, <http://news.softpedia.com/news/Jay-Z-To-Rap-for-Water-Crisis-Awareness-32506.shtml> (February 11, 2009).

Further **Reading**

Books

Burns, Kate, ed. *Rap Music and Culture.* Farmington Hills, Mich.: Greenhaven Press, 2008.

Collins, Tracy Brown. *Missy Elliott.* New York: Chelsea House, 2007.

Orr, Tamra. *Ice Cube: A Blue Banner Biography.* Hockessin, Del.: Mitchell Lane Publishers, 2006.

Simons, Rae. *Kanye West.* Broomall, Penn.: Mason Crest, 2007.

Web Sites

BET—Black Entertainment TV's Web site has the latest news on African-American music, movie, and television stars.
<http://www.bet.com>

Vibe Magazine—Vibe is a publication about music, celebrities, and urban life. Its writers cover rap music and culture.
<http://www.vibe.com>

Index